CONT

A WORLD AT WAR

The Second World War is known as one of the biggest and deadliest wars of all time. It was called a world war because by the time it ended, more than 50 countries had joined the fighting. The Second World War officially began on 3 September 1939, after Germany **invaded** Poland. However, the build-up to the war started in the early 1930s.

Many countries, including Germany, were poor in the 1930s. In Germany, people were frustrated by the government and wanted change. Adolf Hitler and his **Nazi** party rose to power. Hitler persuaded his followers to blame Jewish people for the problems Germany was facing. Nazi forces began to **persecute** and attack Jewish people. By the end of the war in 1945, six million Jews and millions of other people were murdered by Nazi forces. This mass killing is known as the **Holocaust**.

Hitler wanted to make Germany the biggest and most powerful country in Europe. By 1938, his army had already successfully invaded Austria and part of Czechoslovakia (now the Czech Republic).

People in other countries in Europe feared the Nazis would invade them too.

The main countries involved in the Second World War were:

- The **Axis** powers: Germany, Italy and Japan
- The **Allies**: France, Great Britain, the United States, Russia and China

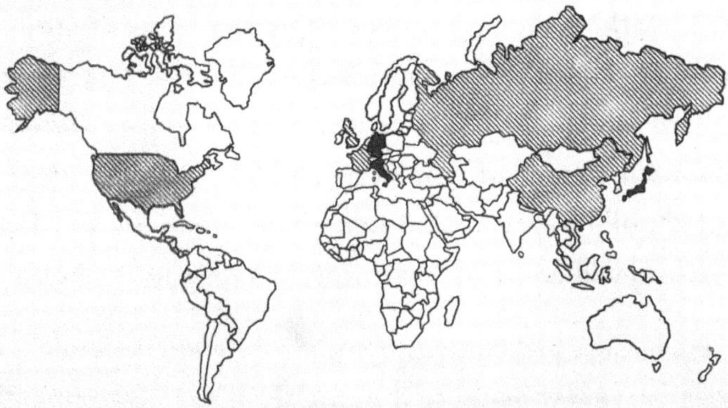

The threat of war and a Nazi invasion was all over the news in Britain. The British government made detailed plans to protect Britain. One of the government's worries was that the German army would launch **air raids** and drop poisonous gas on cities to hurt ordinary people. Many people became Air Raid **Precaution** (ARP) wardens. They were trained to take charge and prepare people in case an air raid happened.

Ordinary people up and down the country were talking about the threat of war. In this book, we look at the diary of a boy called George who was growing up in London in the 1930s, when the war started.

2 September 1938

Dear Diary

It is my ninth birthday today. I had a new yoyo and a toy army tank. Mum made me a cake with candles and gave me a diary with my name, George, on the front of it. Nothing much has ever happened in my life so I never bothered with a diary before, but now there seems to be a lot going on. The newspapers are full of stories about the threat of attack by the Nazi German army and it's all Mum and Dad talk about. Mum doesn't think anything will come of it and says it's all a lot of hot air.

The weirdest present was a gas mask. Well, it wasn't really a present because it came from the government – it just happened to arrive on my birthday. There are

posters all over town telling us to carry our gas masks with us wherever we go. We have to be ready to put them over our faces to stop us breathing in poisonous gases if the German army drops gas over us. It's a pretty scary-looking thing but Mum doesn't think we'll ever have to use them.

Dad doesn't say much but I think he's worried we will go to war. He has a weak heart so he cannot train to be a soldier. He has **volunteered** to be an ARP warden. He's learning to try to protect people if enemy planes drop bombs on London. He would have to report the bombing and tell people what they should do and where they should go to keep safe. Mum says he looks silly in the ARP hat but she smiles when she says it so I think she's secretly proud of him ...

The heavy, steel helmets wardens wear are designed to protect their heads from falling bricks, flying rubble and glass if a bomb dropped.

The British government put a lot of air raid precautions in place. They set up shelters where people could go to be safe from bombs and they trained wardens to lead people to the shelters if there was an air raid.

There were different kinds of shelters. Schools, hospitals and other big buildings often had basements that could be used as shelters. Public air raid shelters were built from brick with concrete roofs. Factories and offices had their own outdoor shelters, with rows of seats for workers and pupils to sit on inside them.

Some people had Morrison shelters inside their homes. These had a steel top that could be used as a table, and wire mesh panels around the four sides, with an entry door through one of the panels. People with outside spaces were offered kits to build Anderson shelters in back yards and gardens.

EYEWITNESS ACCOUNT

"We'd turned the dining room table into a Morrison shelter. It was supposed to protect us from the effects of a bomb blast but people said they weren't very good if the house was hit."

David, who was a child during the Second World War

THE ANDERSON SHELTER

The first Anderson shelter was built in 1939. Anderson shelters were designed to provide some cover against bombs, although they were not able to save people inside if there was a direct hit.

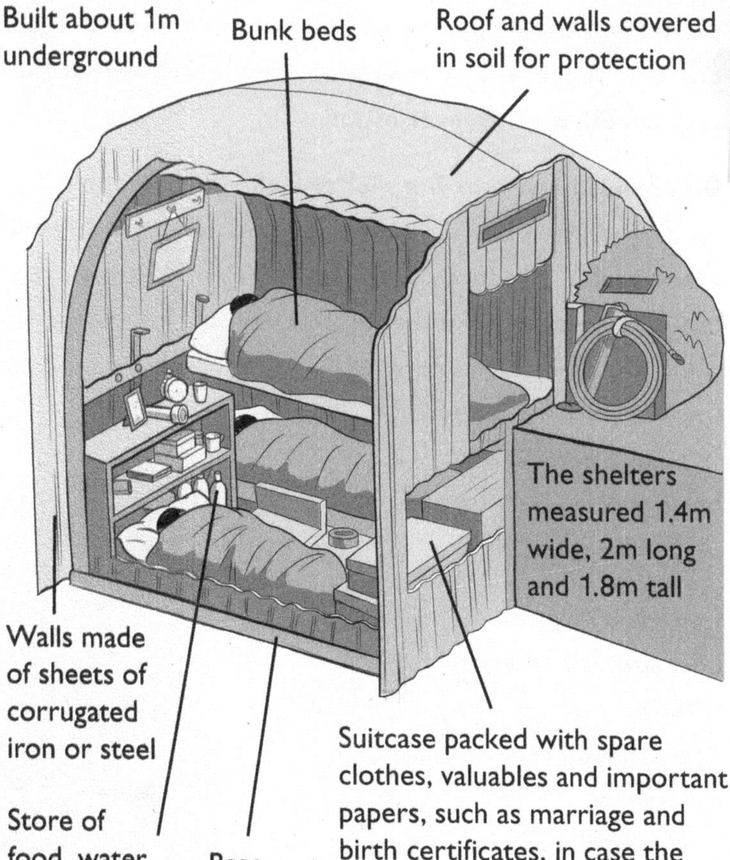

4 August 1939

Dear Diary

Today was a good day. Our new Anderson shelter kit arrived and Mum and Dad let me help them build it. First we had to dig a big hole in the garden. The shelter had to be buried halfway under the ground. Then we built the shelter with steel panels curved into a semi-circular shape and held together by strong bolts. Finally we covered the shelter with a thick layer of soil.

Dad complained that the shelter looked ugly in the garden, so Mum and I are going to grow some flowers and vegetables in the earth covering the roof. That'll make it less of an eyesore. The shelter isn't very big but should fit Mum and Dad, Gran and Grandad and me inside. It's like a den in the back garden and I've always wanted a den.

Some people around here aren't bothering with the shelters. They don't think a real war will happen.

In the six months after war was declared, there was almost no fighting and no bombs were dropped. This period became known as the Phoney War. Many people started to feel that war was never going to happen. They even stopped carrying their gas masks.

Then, in spring 1940, Adolf Hitler sent the German air force (*Luftwaffe*) to attack the British Royal Air Force (RAF). Hitler's plan was to send ships carrying German soldiers to Britain and he didn't want the RAF to be able to sink those ships. The RAF fought back in what became known as the Battle of Britain. Even though the RAF had far fewer planes than the Luftwaffe, the Germans were unable to overcome Britain's air defenses. After the Battle of Britain ended on 31 October 1940, the Nazis decided to increase attacks on London and other British cities.

"Never in the field of human conflict was so much owed by so many to so few ..."

Winston Churchill, Britain's wartime prime minister, speaking about the way the pilots flying relatively small numbers of British planes defeated the many German planes.

THE LONDON BLITZ

On 7 September 1940, the first large-scale night raid on London took place. It was too easy for British forces to shoot down the German bomber planes when they attacked during daylight, so the German army switched to night attacks instead. The nighttime air raids became known as the Blitz, from the German word *Blitzkrieg*, which means 'lightning war'. The bombs lit up the night sky and looked like flashes of lightning. They also came thick and fast!

EYEWITNESS ACCOUNT

"The entire area around the docks was on fire. The bombs just kept on coming. It felt endless. The ground under our feet shook with each explosion and the sky glowed with an eerie, orange light."

George Brown, 30-year-old firefighter in London

Most of the worst-damaged homes were near the docks. The bombers were trying to hit the navy ships moored there. Some bombs started fires and others reduced entire streets to rubble.

GERMAN BOMBS

The German Luftwaffe used different bombs during night raids. They wanted to cause devastation and destruction, and to scare the British people into **surrendering**.

INCENDIARY BOMB

The first planes in a nighttime air raid often dropped **incendiary** or firebombs. Firebombs did not explode. They started deadly fires unless they were put out immediately. The glow from the fires also helped German bomber pilots see where to drop the more powerful high-explosive bombs.

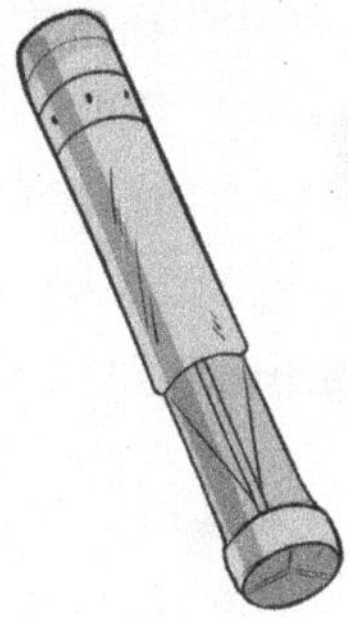

HIGH-EXPLOSIVE BOMB

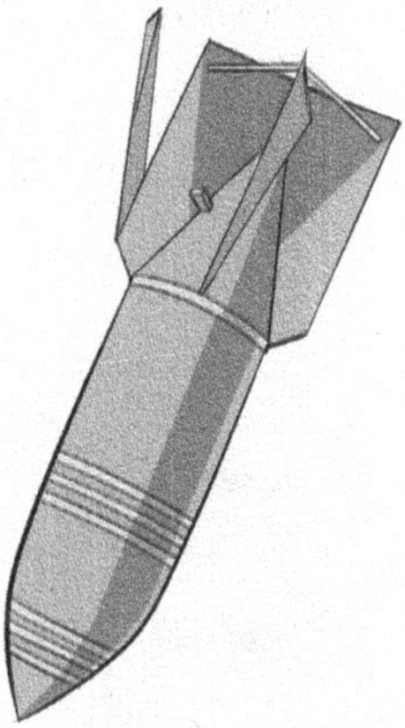

High-explosive bombs injured and killed a lot of people because, when they hit a building, they sent showers of concrete, bricks, glass and other debris flying quickly through the air in all directions. Some of these bombs were enormous. The 1800kg version was 3.75m long. It was nicknamed Hermann after Hermann Göring, the leader of the Luftwaffe.

BLACKOUTS

To save lives during the Blitz, the government introduced nighttime **blackouts**. Street lights were turned off or covered, and people used heavy curtains, cardboard and paint to stop light escaping from buildings after sunset. The idea of the blackout was to stop enemy bomber planes using lights to see where to drop their bombs on streets and houses. During an air raid, all lights had to be turned off. People could be fined if they did not cover their windows properly.

Cars had to partly cover their headlights so that only three narrow slits of light got through. To help drivers and pedestrians see in the dark, the edges of pavements, car bumpers and street furniture like telephone kiosks, lamp-posts or letter boxes were painted white. Even with these precautions, car accidents increased and the number of people killed on the roads almost doubled.

8 September 1940

Dear Diary

Dad was on duty tonight. After the door closed behind him, I heard him knock loudly at Mrs Jordan's, three doors down. She never pulls her curtains properly during a blackout. I don't think she realises she could be helping enemy bombers see where to drop their bombs! She could be fined for not following the rules, but Dad is so soft he'll probably let her off with a warning. I'd like to go out with him on his rounds, but he says it's too dangerous on the roads during blackouts!

It made me jump out of my skin when the air raid **siren** went off. I don't think I'll ever get used to that howling sound. Mum and I stopped making supper and raced down the garden into the Anderson shelter. I'm in here now writing my diary by lamplight. I hate it in here. It's not half as much fun as I thought it'd be. It's so small, cold and damp and it's full of creepy-crawlies. An earwig actually crawled into my ear! Yuk! One night we were stuck in here for eight hours. I hope we're not in here that long tonight. We left Mr Puff our cat outside and I'm really worried about him.

The worst thing of all is that the shelter isn't soundproof. It's impossible to sleep because you can clearly hear all of the chaos of the air raid outside. You can tell when a bomber plane is overhead. Their engines make a loud droning sound. Then you hear a weird whistling noise as a bomb drops. We can only hope it falls far away from us. There's also that rat-a-tat-tat of the anti-aircraft guns shooting at the German army. I don't think they hit many, but at least we're fighting back!

SIRENS AND SHELTERS

When German bomber planes were spotted heading for a city, air raid sirens sounded to warn people to go to a shelter. The siren's rising and falling noise earned it the nickname 'Wailing Winnie' or 'Moaning Minnie'! When the siren went off, people flooded out of their workplaces, schools and homes into shelters. They sometimes stayed there for many hours, until an ARP warden rang a brass hand bell or a continuous siren gave the All Clear signal. These sounds told people the danger had passed.

In London, around 200,000 people took shelter in the Underground stations. Some stations had bunk beds and portable toilets people could use, but there were often not enough to go around.

EYEWITNESS ACCOUNT

"I hated using the Underground stations during an air raid. The smell down there was horrible. I don't know how people could stand it. There were so many people in a closed space with no fresh air and no proper toilets. I didn't even think they were safe!"

May Provis, who was a child during the Second World War

CITIES FIGHT BACK

Cities under attack used different means of defence. At night, **searchlights** shone powerful beams of light that acted like giant torches sweeping back and forth across the dark night sky. When the searchlights showed up a German bomber plane, guns on the ground fired at it. These were known as anti-aircraft weapons.

Barrage balloons were huge silver balloons as big as a house, and filled with gas. They were held in place by heavy steel cables that were strong enough to destroy any aircraft that flew into them. Barrage balloons were used to stop German planes flying low over a city and dropping bombs. They forced German pilots to fly higher, and that made their bombing less accurate.

Some people gave their local barrage balloons nicknames, such as Barry the Barrage Balloon!

AFTER AN AIR RAID

ARP wardens were often the first people out and about after an air raid. They checked people were safe, and rescued people from the rubble of their homes. They gave first aid to anyone who was injured. Ambulances and fire brigades rushed around the towns and cities trying to save lives and homes too. As people came out of their shelters, they were often scared to see what damage had been done to their homes and streets. They were anxious to find family members who may not have been in the same shelter as them during a raid.

This map shows some of the places that suffered the most damage during the Blitz. Bombing started in Coventry and Liverpool in August 1940 and then spread to other cities that had docks, or factories making war planes or weapons, too. Large-scale bombing started in London in September 1940.

9 September 1940

Dear Diary

The German army has been dropping bombs night after night, but last night the sound of the bombs was deafening. We even felt the ground shake! When we heard the All Clear and came out of the shelter, we had a real shock. All of the houses on the opposite side of the street, the lot, were blown apart – there wasn't a house standing. The tiles on the roofs were all gone, curtains were shredded by flying glass, the doors and windows were missing, and there were just piles of rubble. The tears were rolling down from my eyes.

As the dust settled, people began to clear up after the bombing. I heard stories of people with terrible injuries from falling bricks and flying glass who had to be helped. Firemen were damping down the fires. I saw some men tunnelling through the wreckage of a nearby bomb-hit home to rescue people who were trapped under the rubble. Even though it was so awful, everyone was very cheerful, and it felt quite exciting too. Oh, and we found Mr Puff safe and sound as well!

Later in the day, I met up with two friends and we went collecting **shrapnel**. All of the kids do it round here.

When shells from the anti-aircraft guns explode high in the sky, they scatter small jagged pieces of steel that land across the city. We swap pieces and it's fun to show off our collections. I wasn't allowed to stay out long though. Mum is getting more and more worried about me being out and about in case there's an unexpected air raid ...

LEAVING THE CITY

The government was worried that thousands of children could be killed by bombs during the Blitz. So, it decided to send them away from cities to places in the countryside where there were far fewer bombings. This was called **evacuation**.

The first evacuation took place on 1 September 1939, two days before war was declared. Within three days, 1.5 million children had left their parents and their homes. The government did not force parents to send children away, but used leaflets and posters to warn them that evacuated children would be safer.

"Of course it means heartache to be separated from your children, but you can be quite sure that they will be well looked after... You cannot wish, if it is possible to evacuate them, to let your children experience the dangers and fears of air attack in crowded cities."

From a government leaflet entitled 'Evacuation: Why and How?' from July, 1939

Many children remained in the cities, and almost half the children evacuated in September were brought home again by Christmas 1939. This was because during the so-called Phoney War, many parents started to think the cities were safe after all. Then the Blitz began, and many people were killed by the nightly air raids. Evacuations restarted in the summer and autumn of 1940.

The evacuations involved thousands of people. Teachers, local officials, railway staff and many thousands of volunteers helped organise the trips. Some children went to live with relatives, but most went to live with strangers. Some children were even sent abroad to places like Canada, South Africa, Australia and New Zealand. Government evacuations to other countries stopped when German submarines launched **torpedoes** that sank one of the ships carrying **evacuees** to Canada. Seventy-seven out of the ninety children on board died.

30 September 1940

Dear Diary

After many nights of heavy bombing, Mum decided it was too dangerous for me to go on living in a big city during the war. I tried to argue with her, but she just cried and said there was no choice, so I guess I'm stuck with it.

Saying goodbye to Mum and Dad at Paddington Station was horrible. We were all crying, even my dad, and I'd never seen him cry before. I had my suitcase and a label attached to me as if I were a parcel. There was a crowd of kids all waiting at the railway station. We had no idea where we were going, what we would be doing or when we would be coming back. I've never been away from Mum and Dad before. Although a little part of me was excited to be going on an adventure and seeing somewhere new, I also felt scared.

After we set off on the train, some of the kids were still a bit quiet and weepy. Some of the younger children thought they'd been sent away for being naughty and they cried for ages. But there was also a buzz of excitement in the air and a lot of us were chattering about where we thought we'd end up. We sang songs to cheer up the smaller children too.

We travelled in cream and brown carriages pulled by a steam train that puffed and roared. The journey felt like it took all day. It was quite boring most of the way, but after we passed Exeter the scenery changed. We went in and out of rocky tunnels along the coast, which was exciting as I'd never seen the sea before. And in Devon the colour of the soil in the fields is red not brown! It was like a different world ...

PACKING FOR EVACUATION

Parents were given a list of what their children should take with them when they were evacuated.

- Every child wore a big label with their name and other details written on it.
- They all carried their gas mask in its box.
- Their case included items the government told them to bring: a change of underclothes, night clothes, plimsolls or slippers, spare stockings or socks, a toothbrush, a comb, towel, soap, face cloth, handkerchiefs and a warm coat or mackintosh. Each child should bring a packet of food for the day.
- Each child was given a blank postcard to send to their parents to tell them where they were after they were assigned a **host** family.

EVACUEES GET A NEW HOME

The children who were evacuated were sent to live with families in parts of the country that were considered safer, like villages in the countryside. People in the country were told they had to take in the evacuees. Families who took in evacuees were given money by the government. When evacuee children arrived at their destination, **billeting officers** were the people in charge of finding them homes.

Sometimes the billeting officer matched hosts with evacuees. The officer might walk around a village dropping children off with their host families. If a host refused to take a child, they could be fined. In some places, people came and chose children to take with them. In those cases, people sometimes picked children who would be most useful to them. For example, farmers chose strong-looking boys.

2 October 1940

Dear Diary

When the train arrived in Kingsbridge it was late, and we were tired and hungry. Some lady volunteers and a police officer met us at the railway station. They walked us to a church hall. We were given some food and we slept that night on the floor of the church hall. The next morning, a billeting officer came and then people who were going to look after us children came too. They chose which children they wanted to stay with them. Then the children went off one by one with the people who were going to look after them.

I waited – and waited. At first, it seemed as though nobody wanted to take me in. Then Mrs Tucker said she'd be glad to have me. She was old enough to be my gran, I thought, but she seemed nice enough. She had a lovely smile and looked very kind.

It turns out she is a farmer's wife. When we got to the farm, she gave me lemonade and biscuits and took me out to meet Mr Tucker. They have no children of their own and he seemed pleased to have me, too. He promised to teach me lots of things about farming. He said if I wanted to, I could even learn how to bring the cows in for milking. I can't wait to do that!

I have a cosy bedroom all to myself, and Mrs Tucker gave me extra blankets to keep me warm as it's a bit cold in the farmhouse. I think I'm going to like it here. Even so, when I came to my bed last night, I felt sad. I'm so worried about Mum and Dad being in London at the mercy of the German bombers, and I feel very homesick. I'm not ashamed to admit I cried myself to sleep.

LIFE IN THE COUNTRY

It took a while for many of the evacuated children and their host families to get used to each other. Some children were placed with families who lived on farms several miles from the nearest village. They had only cold water that had to be pumped up to the kitchen and outside toilets. Some country homes didn't have electricity. Many evacuees were surprised by how quiet it was in the countryside and how little there was going on compared to the city.

On the other hand, some host families were surprised that their evacuee children had never seen a vegetable before. They believed city folk must have very poor diets. They were also shocked that some of the children were dirty and knew swear words.

Some hosts wrote letters to officials complaining about the state or behaviour of the child staying with them, and some evacuee children ran away from their hosts.

FOOD RATIONS

One good thing about living in the countryside was that there was more food to eat than in cities. Farmers grew fruit and vegetables and kept cows for milk, butter and cheese. At this time, food was **rationed**, which meant people could have only a small amount of certain foods every week. Before the war, Britain had **imported** around two-thirds of its food from abroad. German attacks stopped British ships bringing this food to Britain. Rationing was a way to make sure everyone could still get enough food.

Everyone had their own ration book with **coupons** in it. When people bought and paid for food such as butter, tea and meat, the shopkeeper would cut out or scribble on coupons so they couldn't be used again.

Children had a blue ration book, and they were allowed more milk and fruit than adults. The shortage of sugar meant that children did not have many sweets, cakes or biscuits.

8 October 1940

Dear Diary

I love sitting in the farm kitchen. There's a big fire in there and it always smells of freshly baked bread and cooking. We had rabbit pie for supper tonight. Mr Tucker catches the rabbits himself. Then we had blackberry and apple crumble with fruit that I helped Mrs Tucker pick from the hedges along the lane. I'd never picked blackberries before. They stained my fingers purple, and I got a few scratches from the thorns, but it was fun being outside. Tomorrow Mrs Tucker's going to show me how to make butter and cheese.

Mr Tucker has shown me how to do some of the jobs around the farm already. I've been collecting the eggs from the henhouses and feeding and giving water to the hens. I thought the hens were like pets and I had started to give them all names and grow quite fond of them. Then Mr Tucker killed and plucked one of the hens for our supper yesterday! I was a bit upset, but I like eating chicken for dinner, so I guess I have to get used to this new way of life.

The farmhouse is very cold, but tonight I had a warm bath in a big tin bath that Mr Tucker carried in. He sat it in front of the living room fire. Mrs Tucker boiled several kettles of water to get enough for me to sit in it, but it was lovely and warm. I know I'm lucky that Mr and Mrs Tucker are so kind. I've heard tales from other evacuees at school who complain that their hosts treat them like servants!

DIG FOR VICTORY

Evacuated children were not the only ones who found themselves having to adapt to a new life in the countryside. During the war, farms needed to grow more food, and farmers were asked to grow or produce twice as much food as they had done before the war started. Growing more food meant more workers were needed, and this was at a time when many male farm workers aged 21 and over had been called up to join the fighting in the war. Women from towns and cities across the UK volunteered to leave home to work on farms all over the country.

The volunteers were part of the Women's Land Army (WLA). These women became known as Land Girls.

EYEWITNESS ACCOUNT

"Most of the Land Girls I knew lived in hostels. We all had to be fast learners on the farms we worked on and do anything that was needed on the land. We learned to milk cows, clean out cow sheds, feed chickens and plant cabbages, broccoli and lots of other vegetables."

Edith Taylor, a Land Girl who worked in Devon

THE WOMEN'S LAND ARMY

The WLA trained women to do all kinds of farm work, such as weeding, ploughing, picking fruit and vegetables, milking cows, looking after farm animals and driving tractors. Some Land Girls were even trained to be rat catchers to stop rats damaging or eating food supplies and animal feed on farms.

Some land girls lived in groups in hostels, and worked on different farms. The hostels were often old country houses or other large buildings. Other Land Girls lived on the farm where they worked. Around 17,000 women joined the WLA when the war started, with as many as 80,000 joining up before it ended.

Land Girls had a uniform including trousers, an overall coat and boots so they could move freely to do practical tasks like driving a tractor.

15 October 1940

Dear Diary

Farmer Tucker has taught me how to bring the cows in for morning milking at last! I have to walk to the end of the field and shout: "Cow! Cow! Cow!" So long as I say it loudly enough, the cows all start marching across the field. Then I walk them down the lane to the barn.

Mr Tucker was telling me about a farmer who lives nearby, who has painted white stripes on his cows to stop them getting run over if they wander into the road during a blackout! Mr Tucker was laughing and saying that farmer wouldn't need to paint his cows if he mended his fences – then the cows couldn't wander off and make a nuisance of themselves.

I've also made friends with Betty Stewart, a Land Girl who works on the farm. She helps Mr Tucker plant fields full of potatoes. She likes the Tuckers too. She says they treat her like a daughter. Some Land Girls who she knows have to eat separately from the family they live with, and they are made to feel very unwelcome.

She told me that some local people are rude about the uniform that she has to wear. Around here, women even wear skirts when they're riding a horse, but Betty loves wearing trousers. She says they're much better for working in! I feel like she understands what it's been like for me. It's the first time she's left home too, as she's only 17. I think it's taken a while for local people to see she's a nice person and a hard worker, and it's taken me a while to settle in to school too.

SCHOOL AND DAILY LIFE

During the war, many schools were forced to close. One in five schools was destroyed by bombs, and some schools were shut so they could be used as air raid warden stations. Some children had lessons in unusual places such as pubs and churches, or even outdoors. Lessons were often disturbed by air raids. As well as losing out on education, children from poor families also suffered because they no longer got the free milk and lunches they used to be given at school.

The schools that remained open did not have enough staff, because thousands of male teachers were called up to fight in the war. There was also a shortage of books and other equipment. Teachers who were left had to teach bigger classes, with fewer materials like paper and pencils.

School lessons were often different too. Some boys and girls had knitting classes. They learned to knit socks or scarves for soldiers.

GAS MASK DRILLS

Some schools held **drills** every day. Children were trained to put their gas masks on, and go quickly but carefully to a safe area or a shelter. A teacher would suddenly shout: "Gas, gas!" and children would race to put on their masks. Sometimes the children were timed and encouraged to improve on how fast and well they did this.

EYEWITNESS ACCOUNT

"I dreaded gas drills at school. The masks were made from black rubber, with a clear plastic part over your face and a huge filter over your mouth. The rubber smell was really strong and the masks made us all look like scary pigs!"

Reginald Butcher, who was evacuated to Wales when he was 10.

The lower part of the gas mask was a tin can with tiny holes in it. It contained a block of asbestos – a chemical substance that can absorb poisonous gases. Children breathed in clean air through the tin and breathed out through the rubber flap.

25 October 1940

Dear Diary

I have to walk to school most days no matter what the weather is like, but I don't mind that. The school is in an old building with one big classroom. There are so many of us in each class, there is hardly room for us all. There is only one teacher for all of us. There are hardly any books, so we all have to share. If we do any writing, it is on scrap paper.

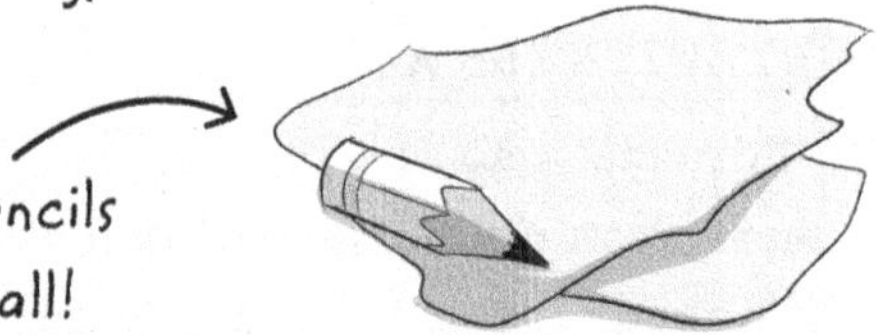

We have to use our pencils until they are very small!

Yesterday, the teacher asked me to describe life in London. The local children's eyes nearly popped out of their heads when I told them about the nightly air raids, the noise of the bombings and some of the destruction I had seen. They could scarcely believe it!

But later that day, some of the kids started teasing me about the way I talk. They say that I sound funny. I told them it's the Devon way of speaking that sounds silly, and they didn't like that one bit. Some of them seem to blame us evacuees for making them have to squash up in the classrooms, too.

Today was a better day. For a start, I got a ride to school in the milk lorry. The driver offered me a lift after he had collected the milk from the farm. Then at school, I made some friends. We had a gas mask drill and I made some of the children laugh by making a 'raspberry' noise every time I breathed out through it. I know it was naughty because it used to drive Mum mad when I did it. The teacher told me off, so I won't do it again, but it was worth it as now I've got some friends to play with at breaktime.

DAILY LIFE

The war had a big impact on everyone, but in some ways daily life continued as it had always done. Even if people had to spend the nights in an air raid shelter in the city, they got up and went to work again as usual the next day.

During the day, when there was no school and no air raids, children in the countryside and the cities played outside with their friends, riding bikes, climbing trees, skipping and sometimes playing war games. There were no new toys, so on rainy days, children read old books, did colouring on scrap paper or played board games.

In the evenings, families often sat together to listen to the radio to hear the latest news about the war and to enjoy music or comedy shows. People also watched news reports and films at the cinema. Most films were in black and white, though some were in colour.

Children evacuated to the countryside kept in touch with their families back home by letters. Many children eagerly awaited the post bringing them news from home and to find out if their parents, pets and homes had survived the bombings.

HELPING THE WAR EFFORT

Children also did activities to help Britain in the war. As well as knitting scarves and socks for soldiers, many children helped to grow vegetables at home and school. Older boys and girls joined the Boy Scouts and Girl Guides. They helped air raid wardens by running across cities carrying messages or looking out for fires. Younger children helped to collect waste paper or materials that could be recycled into useful equipment needed for the war. Some children helped to collect aluminium metal pots and pans so these could be used to make aircraft!

As there were no new toys during the war, some children often made their own toys out of wood – or they collected old broken bicycles and prams to make new bikes or carts.

31st December 1940

Dear Diary

Most weekends I help out with farm work on Saturdays, and then on Sundays we go to church in the morning. We often go for a walk in the countryside too, and last weekend we went a long way. We went as far as the beach. It was a very long beach, but we could only stay in an area close to the rocks. The rest of the beach had a **barbed wire** fence all along it! Mr Tucker said this was to stop German boats landing here, full of soldiers trying to invade. It was very cold, so we didn't stay long.

We usually go to the cinema once a month for a treat. Unfortunately, we can't go this week because a bomb dropped in town and blew the doors off the cinema! I wasn't disappointed though, because we had a Christmas party in the village hall. All the children from school came. There was music and party games and a table full of food. Every child was given an orange as an extra special treat.

This is the first Christmas I have ever spent away from Mum and Dad. They sent me presents of some chocolate, a comic and a wooden war plane that Dad made for me himself. Mum sent me a long letter too. She said that the

people who went to the Underground during air raids held Christmas parties and sang Christmas carols together. They even hung streamers on the walls! She said she and Dad and Mr Puff spent Christmas Eve in the air raid shelter in the garden. It sounded very lonely. It was very strange not to see them. It made me feel more homesick than ever.

HOME AGAIN ...

The air raids lasted over eight months. London was bombed the most, but the Blitz was a long and deadly attack on cities and towns, big ports, factories and warehouses across the UK.

The biggest and worst air raid of the Blitz on London happened between 11pm on 10 May and 6am on 11 May 1941. It was a night of a full moon, which helped to light the way for over 500 enemy planes. It was also a low tide, which meant that there wasn't much water in the River Thames for firefighters to use to put out the blazes caused by incendiary bombs. The night of 10 to 11 May became known as the Hardest Night.

The Hardest Night was also the last air raid of the Blitz. On 11 May 1941, Adolf Hitler decided to stop sending planes to carry out air raids on Britain. He sent the planes to join German soldiers invading Russia instead. The nighttime bombings of the main Blitz were over at last!

BLITZ CASUALTIES

By the time the Blitz ended:

- over 40,000 British people had been killed, about half of them in London alone
- around 140,000 people had been injured
- around 2 million homes had been destroyed, 60% of which were in London.

Even though the government encouraged people to leave their children in the countryside until after the war ended, some parents brought their children home after the Blitz stopped.

When evacuees got home, they found the cities much changed. In London, many famous buildings had been bombed, including Buckingham Palace, the Houses of Parliament and the Tower of London. In some places, whole areas of the city were so badly damaged that they had to be almost completely rebuilt.

22 June 1941

Dear Diary

Well, it finally happened. I'm back in London with Mum and Dad. It was sad leaving Mr and Mrs Tucker. They were so kind to me, and I loved working on the farm. I promised I'll come back to visit them when the war is over, and I truly hope I can keep that promise.

London looks so different from what I remember. Whole streets have disappeared and there are piles of rubble where entire buildings were before. It feels very dusty compared to the countryside. In some places, there are huge dips in the ground called craters where bombs went off.

Mum made me a new pair of shorts from some old fabric she came across, as a homecoming present. She couldn't make me a pair of trousers because boys still have to wear shorts to save material. She made them big so they'll last me longer too! Clothing is rationed because fabric is needed for uniforms, and factory workers are making other things like weapons instead. People are mending their old clothes and trying to buy new clothes only if they really need them.

Mum is now a volunteer with the Women's Voluntary Service. During the Blitz, she helped to provide drinks and meals to the ARP wardens, firefighters and other workers. Now she goes out helping people in different ways. She helps run a clothes swap, where people can bring clothes that their children have grown out of, and swap them for bigger clothes.

There are no more air raids at the moment and that's a big relief. But the country is still at war. I wonder if life will ever get back to normal?

THE BABY BLITZ

After the Blitz ended in summer 1941, life was much safer for ordinary people living in Britain. There were a few air raids, but nothing like the bombing attacks that happened during the Blitz. This changed on the evening of 22 January 1944, when more than 400 bomber planes attacked London without warning. It was a huge air raid that rained down high explosive and incendiary bombs on the city. Attacks on cities including Bristol, Hull and Cardiff went on from January to May 1944, a time that people nicknamed the Baby Blitz or the Little Blitz.

TAKING REVENGE

Hitler ordered the Luftwaffe to start bombing cities in Britain again because he wanted revenge. Since 1942, RAF planes had been making raids on German cities. For example, in 1943, nighttime air raids on the German city of Hamburg destroyed more than half the city, killed around 50,000 people and left nearly a million people homeless.

THE TERROR OF THE BUZZ BOMBS

During the Baby Blitz, over 1500 people were killed and around 3000 people were badly injured in air raids across Britain. From June 1944, the German army started using a different means of attack – V-1 and, later, V-2 bombs were not dropped from planes driven by pilots. They were flying bombs, fired from secret launch sites in northern Europe. The V-1s were nicknamed buzz bombs or doodlebugs because they sounded like flying insects.

The V-1 and V-2 weapons were so dangerous and destructive that a million women, children, and elderly and disabled people were evacuated from London. These flying bombs killed over 30,000 ordinary British people and left hundreds of thousands homeless.

The V-2s were powered by a rocket engine and were as tall as a four-storey building.

EYEWITNESS ACCOUNT

"I remember watching the doodlebugs come over and praying that they wouldn't stop and drop on us. We all held our breath until they went past. If a doodlebug stopped and dropped, all you could do was run and hope that it wasn't coming near you."

Ethel Corby, an evacuee who returned to London in 1941

28 March 1944

Dear Diary

We all thought we'd seen the last of the German bombs here in London when the Blitz ended, but unfortunately it turns out we were wrong. The Baby Blitz was bad, but luckily none of the bombs that dropped in those nighttime air raids landed near our street. Now the German army are sending doodlebugs!

The doodlebugs are powered by jet engines and they sound like a noisy motorbike. They keep flying until they run out of fuel. Then they drop from the air and explode wherever they land. Whenever we hear a doodlebug, we all stand still and just watch it until it has safely passed us by. They're very scary! It's comforting to hear the sounds of the anti-aircraft guns firing at them. Dad told me that we're managing to shoot down more than three-quarters of the nasty things.

We're all getting really fed up with the blackouts too. It'll be alright in summer when it stays light until late, but spending hours in darkness is miserable. Dad says lots of people aren't bothering to follow blackout rules any more, especially now that the flying bombs are here. They don't have pilots who follow street or house lights, so blackouts won't stop them!

When I'm not in school or with my friends, I'm busy in the back garden. Since working on the farm, Mum and Dad have said I can take over the vegetable patch. I grow lots of vegetables to eat or share with our neighbours. Mum hasn't got time, and she spends hours queuing up to buy food rations in the shops. I'm growing a lot of carrots because Mum and I make a tasty carrot and chocolate pudding – I know it sounds odd, but it's delicious!

THE END OF THE WAR

The attacks on London by V-1 and V-2 flying bombs and rockets ended in March 1945. Not long after, on 7 May 1945, Germany surrendered. The British leader Winston Churchill announced it on 8 May, which was named Victory in Europe Day or **VE Day**. Japan did not surrender until 2 September 1945, after **atomic bombs** were dropped on the Japanese cities of Hiroshima and Nagasaki in August.

8 May 1945

Dear Diary

People everywhere are waving Union Jack flags and singing and dancing. Kids have made a lot of the flags using cardboard and crayons. I've never seen anything like it. Dad says people are having street parties all over Britain to celebrate that, after nearly six long years, the war in Europe is over. Yippee!

In our street, everybody put together all their best rations so we could celebrate VE Day in style. There was a big table in the street and lots of folk made paper hats. I even made a hat for Mr Puff! The parties didn't stop when it got dark. People made a big bonfire in the middle of the street and everyone danced around it. There was music from a radio and someone played tunes on a banjo. We're all tired now but I can't sleep because I'm so happy. What a day!

GLOSSARY

air raids	attacks in which planes drop bombs from the sky onto targets on the ground
Allies	the group of countries, including the United States, Britain and the Soviet Union (made up of Russia and 14 other countries), who joined in the war against Germany and other Axis countries
atomic bomb	extremely powerful bomb that gets its power by splitting an atom of the element uranium
Axis	the group of countries, including Germany, Italy and Japan, who fought against the Allied countries
barbed wire	wire with sharp points spaced evenly along it and used as a barrier
billeting officer	person whose job it was to find suitable houses and families for evacuees
blackouts	the turning off of all lights in towns and cities
coupons	vouchers or tickets that let you buy something
drills	activities in which you learn a new skill by repeating it several times
evacuation	moving people from a dangerous place to a place where they are safer
evacuees	people who move from a dangerous place to a place where they are safer
Holocaust	the killing of millions of people, mostly Jewish people, by Nazi Germany during the Second World War
hosts	people who welcome guests into their homes
imported	brought goods from abroad
incendiary	bomb used to start fires
invaded	used an army to take over a country
Nazi	a member of the far-right National Socialist German Workers' Party
persecute	hurt or treat someone cruelly or badly because of their race or religious or political beliefs
precaution	an action carried out to stop something unpleasant or dangerous happening
rationed	when something like food is limited so that there is enough for everyone to have some

searchlights lights with a very bright focused beam that can be turned in any direction

shrapnel bits of a bomb, shell or bullet that has exploded

siren device that makes a loud warning noise

surrendering stopping fighting and giving in to an enemy force

torpedoes long, thin bombs that travel underwater to destroy ships or submarines

VE Day stands for Victory in Europe Day; marks the end of the Second World War in Europe on 8 May 1945

volunteered offered to do something without being paid to do it

INDEX

NOW ANSWER THE QUESTIONS ...

1 Why was the war between 1939 and 1945 called a 'world war' (page 2)?

2 Why do you think the author included the diagram on page 7?

3 'This period became known as the Phoney War' (page 9). Think of another word or phrase that could be used instead of 'phoney'.

4 Read page 24. Why was each child given a blank postcard to send to their parents?

5 Why is 'Dig for Victory' on page 32 an appropriate heading for information about growing food?

6 Read pages 34 to 35. What do George and Betty have in common?

7 Give the meaning of the phrase 'war effort' on page 41.

8 Which jobs would you have liked to do to help out with the war effort?